Flavours of Wales

THE SEAWEED COOKBOOK

Gilli Davies and Huw Jones

GRAFFEG

The Seaweed Cookbook
Published in Great Britain in 2016 by
Graffeg Limited

Text by Gilli Davies copyright © 2016.
Photographs by Huw Jones copyright © 2016.
Food styling by André Moore.
Designed and produced by Graffeg Limited
copyright © 2016

Graffeg Limited, 24 Stradey Park Business
Centre, Mwrwg Road, Llangennech, Llanelli,
Carmarthenshire SA14 8YP Wales UK
Tel 01554 824000 www.graffeg.com

ISBN 9781910862032

1 2 3 4 5 6 7 8 9

CONTENTS

Seaweed

Well, did you know they eat seaweed in Wales? Yes, it's true. Seaweed, in the form of boiled *porphyra umbilicalis* or laverbread, has been an important and healthy part of the diet in south Wales since the Romans were here.

Now available in handy tins, it can still be found freshly prepared in the markets of south Wales, and not so long ago vans used to drive up the valleys to take laverbread (bara lawr in Welsh) and cockles to the miners to eat with bacon for their breakfast.

But that's not all. Samphire grows around the coast too and adds that delicious crisp snap of seaside flavour when picked and eaten straight away, or blanched, or combined in clever but simple fish dishes.

Gathering porphyra umbilicalis, or kelp as it is known in other Celtic regions, is not so easy. It is found mainly at low tide, clinging to the exposed rocks and the shiny purplish/green fronds must be pulled off the rocks by hand. After a very serious wash to remove the sand, it is boiled for up to six hours by which time it's a dark green, rather glutinous substance, that has a delicious tang of the sea.

Traditionally laverbread was mixed with oatmeal and fried in bacon fat but today it has become something of a celebrity ingredient in the kitchens of many good cooks and chefs. It now appears on menus in all manner of dishes, from delicious sauces for fish dishes to making a great accompaniment for Welsh salt marsh lamb.

With the developing interest in seaweeds worldwide, Wales can boast a number of entrepreneurs who are developing new ideas to use their native seaweeds. Whether you pop in to the extremely trendy Môr (Welsh for sea) Cafe at Freshwater East to sample delicious dishes such as laverbread pesto, or pick up a bag of Seaweed Snacks made by Selwyns, one of the original laverbread harvesting companies on the Gower, it seems that Welsh seaweed is becoming much more available. And ever more so, with the development of the Swansea barrage, where seaweeds and oyster beds will be developed within the lagoon.

Although seaweeds are generally thought to add a healthy element to our diet, it appears that some are healthier than others. Happily for the Welsh, their laverbread is perfect in every way. It contains a high proportion of protein, iodine in just the right proportion, and vitamin B, B2, A, D and C. It also contains very few calories. No wonder then that it is called Welsh man's caviar.

CRAB AND SEAWEED FISHCAKES

You can use tinned crab and tinned or dried seaweed for these fishcakes, but if you happen to be near a fresh fish stall, so much the better.

CRAB AND SEAWEED FISHCAKES

Ingredients

450g white fish, haddock, cod, coley etc.

225g fresh crabmeat

2 eggs, beaten

150g fresh breadcrumbs

1 tablespoon laverbread or 3 sheets nori, crumbled

Light olive oil for frying

Breadcrumb crust

3 tablespoons dried breadcrumbs

1 egg, beaten

Serves 4

❶ Mix the fish, crabmeat, 2 eggs, fresh breadcrumbs and seaweed together thoroughly. Divide into small patties and place on trays. Cover with greaseproof paper and chill for a couple of hours or overnight.

❷ Brush the fishcakes with the beaten egg and toss them in the dried breadcrumbs.

❸ Shallow fry the fishcakes in hot oil until golden brown on both sides, about 5-6 minutes.

❹ Serve hot with lemon wedges, mayonnaise and a garnish of watercress.

LAVERCAKES
WITH BACON

It sounds a strange mixture, to eat seaweed with bacon, but do try it because you'll understand why it was so popular with the Welsh miners.

LAVERCAKES WITH BACON

Ingredients

8 rashers streaky bacon

100g fresh or tinned laverbread

25g medium or fine oatmeal

1 diced red onion

Serves 4

❶ Dry fry the streaky bacon in a large pan until the fat begins to run. Continue to cook until crisp and then remove from the pan and keep warm.

❷ Mix the laverbread with the oatmeal and onion and shape into little rissole-like cakes about 5cm across and 2cm thick.

❸ Slide the laver cakes into the hot bacon fat and fry fairly quickly for 2 – 3 minutes on each side, shaping and patting the cakes with a palette knife as they fry. Lift out carefully.

PRAWNS WITH PASTA
AND SEAWEED SAUCE

This recipe has always been a favourite with my family who love the combination of flavours and textures.

PRAWNS WITH PASTA AND SEAWEED SAUCE

Ingredients

400g raw king prawns, shelled

200g pasta

175g laverbread

1 clove garlic, crushed

1 dessertspoon olive oil

Splash of white wine

1 heaped teaspoon tomato purée

150ml double cream

Pinch each of salt and freshly grated nutmeg

Serves 4

❶ Cook the pasta in boiling water until al dente and strain.

❷ Fry the crushed garlic in the oil until soft but not brown then add the laverbread, wine, tomato purée, cream and seasoning. Stir well and simmer for 2 minutes

❸ Meanwhile, griddle the prawns quickly until they turn pink.

❹ Combine the pasta with the sauce and prawns and serve immediately.

NOISETTES OF WELSH LAMB WITH LAVER AND ORANGE SAUCE

These noisettes of Welsh lamb are delicious, and with this laver and orange sauce you'll wonder why you never tried it before.

NOISETTES OF WELSH LAMB WITH LAVER AND ORANGE SAUCE

Ingredients

225g laverbread

Grated rind and juice of 1 orange

25g butter

Lamb stock made from boiling some lamb bones with root vegetables and herbs

Salt and freshly ground black pepper

8 – 12 noisettes of lamb, neatly tied, with a thin surround of fat

Serves 4-6

❶ In a small pan, heat the laverbread and fruit juice.

❷ Cook for a few minutes, stirring all the time.

❸ Add the butter little by little until the sauce looks rich and glossy.

❹ Add enough lamb stock to ensure a good pouring consistency.

❺ Season to taste and keep warm.

❻ Heat the grill to its hottest and cook the noisettes, turning once, until they are crisp on the outside but still a little pink in the middle.

❼ Serve the lamb with the sauce separately, with a potch of mashed root vegetables, such as carrot and parsnip or swede, to offset the richness of the laver sauce.

PAN FRIED SCALLOPS
WITH SEAWEED
SAUCE

This dish takes seconds to make so be sure to have all the ingredients ready. You won't want to overcook the scallops for fear that they toughen.

PAN FRIED SCALLOPS WITH SEAWEED SAUCE

Ingredients

450g queen scallops

25g butter

1 tablespoon laverbread (pulped spinach as an alternative)

Grated rind of ½ lemon

1 glass dry white wine (Welsh, if possible)

1 tablespoon double cream or crème fraîche.

Serves 6 as a starter

1. Clean the scallops and dry on kitchen paper. Leave the corals attached wherever possible.

2. In a large frying pan, heat the butter until it sizzles.

3. Toss in the scallops and fry quickly so that they cook on all sides.

4. Remove from the pan and keep warm in six individual serving dishes.

5. Place the laverbread and the lemon rind in the pan with the wine, bring to the boil, taste for seasoning and add the cream or crème fraîche.

6. Pour the sauce over the scallops and serve immediately.

7. Serve with fresh herb rolls or warm herb bread.

SMOKED HADDOCK
AND SAMPHIRE
OMELETTE

Superb crunchy samphire makes this dish very special and combined with smoked haddock and fresh eggs, who could want for more?

SMOKED HADDOCK AND SAMPHIRE OMELETTE

Ingredients

225g naturally smoked haddock

1 tablespoon laverbread (optional)

100g fresh samphire

2 tablespoons double cream

5 eggs

2-3 tablespoons freshly grated Parmesan cheese

salt and pepper

25g butter

Serves 4

❶ Steam or microwave the haddock until just opaque then flake the flesh, removing the skin and bones. Mix the fish with the cream.

❷ Wash the samphire thoroughly, removing any woody stems and cut into 5cm lengths.

❸ Separate the eggs. Beat the yolks together with some salt and pepper. Whisk the egg whites until stiff and fold in with the haddock and half the cheese.

❹ Heat the butter in an omelette or small frying pan. When it stops sizzling, pour in the egg mixture and stir to help it set. Scatter over the samphire, laverbread, if used, and remaining Parmesan and finish cooking until a hot grill.

SMOKED HADDOCK WITH SEAWEED & WELSH RAREBIT CRUST

Well, why not combine two Welsh favourites in one dish? Laverbread and Welsh rarebit go deliciously well together and the addition of the smoked haddock is a bonus.

SMOKED HADDOCK WITH SEAWEED & WELSH RAREBIT CRUST

Ingredients

600g natural smoked haddock fillet, skinned

100g laverbread

Welsh Rarebit

225g strong cheddar

25g butter, melted

50g of laverbread

1 tablespoon English mustard

1 tablespoon flour

4 tablespoons beer

Cayenne pepper

Serves 4

1 Put the haddock in a single layer in a dish. Pour over boiling water, cover and leave the fish to soak for 10 minutes. This will cook it.

2 Mix all the ingredients for the rarebit together.

3 Spread the laverbread across the bottom of a heatproof dish, arrange the drained haddock on top and cover with the rarebit.

4 Leave under a hot grill until the rarebit is bubbling and golden brown.

SIMPLE SMOKED SALMON
AND AVOCADO SUSHI

For centuries the Welsh have been gathering and eating seaweed. Who would have thought that the Japanese were using the very same type of seaweed for their sushi?

SIMPLE SMOKED SALMON AND AVOCADO SUSHI

Ingredients

300g sushi rice

2 tablespoons rice or white wine vinegar

1 teaspoon caster sugar

1 large avocado

juice ½ lemon

4 sheets nori seaweed

4 slices smoked salmon

1 bunch chives

Sweet soy sauce – for serving

Serves 4

❶ Put the rice in a small pan with 600ml water. Bring to the boil and cook for 10 minutes until the water is absorbed and the rice is tender. Stir in the vinegar and sugar, cover and cool.

❷ Skin, stone and slice the avocado. Put in a bowl and squeeze over the lemon juice, turning the avocado to ensure the pieces are covered.

❸ Divide the rice between the nori sheets and spread it out evenly, leaving a 1cm border at the top and bottom. Lay the salmon over the rice, followed by the chives and finally position the avocado across the centre.

❹ Fold the bottom edge of the seaweed over the filling, then roll it up firmly. Dampen the top border with a little water to help it seal the roll. Repeat to make 4 rolls. At this stage, the rolls can be wrapped individually in cling film and chilled until ready to serve.

❺ Using a serrated knife, cut each roll into 8 rounds. Serve with sweet soy sauce for dipping.

DEEP FRIED LAVER SEAWEED

I first ate this crispy seaweed at Fairy Hill Hotel on the Gower where they serve it in the bar before dinner. It's the perfect way to begin a gastronomic evening.

DEEP FRIED LAVER SEAWEED

Ingredients

100g laver seaweed

Flour

Vegetable oil for deep-frying

A good pinch of ground coriander seed and Szechuan pepper

Serves 4

1 Wash the laver seaweed thoroughly to remove the sand.

2 Leave the seaweed to drain in a colander and then dry thoroughly.

3 Tear the laver into strips, dip in flour and shake off the excess. Deep-fry the laver for about 2-3 minutes until crisp.

4 Sprinkle the laver with the coriander and Szechuan pepper. Serve as a nibble with drinks.

SALMON AND
SAMPHIRE ROLLS

Picking samphire along the shore at low tide in Newport Pembrokeshire is one of life's great pleasures. It snaps in your fingers and who can resist a nibble straight away.

SALMON AND SAMPHIRE ROLLS

Ingredients

200g good quality
smoked salmon

100g fresh samphire

450g fresh salmon,
boned and skinless

75g of laverbread

½ glass dry white wine

100g cream cheese

1 tablespoon creamed
horseradish

Good squeeze of
lemon juice

Serves 4

❶ First make the salmon filling: Steam or microwave the fresh salmon in the white wine and leave to cool. Process it with the cream cheese, horseradish, laverbread and lemon to make a smooth pâté. Chill.

❷ Divide the slices of smoked salmon into 8 wide strips and roll each gently around a good dessertspoonful of the pâté.

❸ Wash the samphire well, removing any woody stems and arrange in fronds on serving plates.

❹ Serve two rolls per plate with brown bread and butter or melba toast.

METRIC AND IMPERIAL EQUIVALENTS

Weights	Solid
15g	½oz
25g	1oz
40g	1½oz
50g	1¾oz
75g	2¾oz
100g	3½oz
125g	4½oz
150g	5½oz
175g	6oz
200g	7oz
250g	9oz
300g	10½oz
400g	14oz
500g	1lb 2oz
1kg	2lb 4oz
1.5kg	3lb 5oz
2kg	4lb 8oz
3kg	6lb 8oz

Volume	Liquid
15ml	½ floz
30ml	1 floz
50ml	2 floz
100ml	3½ floz
125ml	4 floz
150ml	5 floz (¼ pint)
200ml	7 floz
250ml	9 floz
300ml	10 floz (½ pint)
400ml	14 floz
450ml	16 floz
500ml	18 floz
600ml	1 pint (20 floz)
1 litre	1¾ pints
1.2 litre	2 pints
1.5 litre	2¾ pints
2 litres	3½ pints
3 litres	5¼ pints

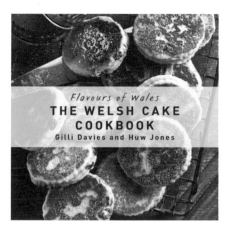
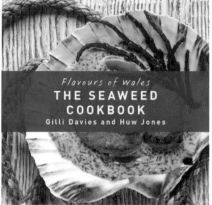
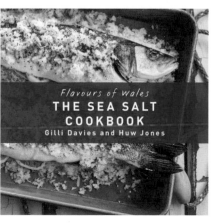

FLAVOURS OF WALES COLLECTION

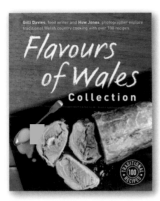

Cook up a Welsh feast with the full *Flavours of Wales* collection in cookbooks, pocket books and notecards to share with friends.

Flavours of Wales Collection book with over 100 recipes by Gilli Davies, photographed by Huw Jones £20.00

10 Recipe Notecards and envelopes in a gift pack. Full recipe inside with space for a message £8.99

Flavours of Wales Collection in a gift slip case with 5 pock books £12.99

Flavours of Wales pocket books £2.99

Available from all good bookshops, kitchen and gift shops and online www.graffeg.com Tel 01554 824000.

GRAFFEG
Books and Gifts from Wales